AUSSIE BIG ACHIEVERS

DYLAN

ALCOTT

written by RICHARD SIMPKIN

illustrated by DEBRA O'HALLORAN

BOOLARONG
PRESS
Established 1976

Other AUSSIE BIG ACHIEVERS books
STEVE IRWIN
CATHY FREEMAN
ASH BARTY
SHANE WARNE

We acknowledge the Traditional Owners of the land on which we publish books, the Quandamooka people, and pay our respects to Elders past, present and emerging.

Disclaimer

The information in this book is true and complete to the best of our knowledge.

All recommendations are made without any guarantee on the part of the author, illustrator and publisher, who also disclaim any liability incurred in connection with the use of this data or specific details.

This publication has not been prepared, approved or licensed by the individual that it has been written about. It also hasn't been approved or licensed by the individual's management. This is not an official publication.

Published by:
Boolarong Press
38/1631 Wynnum Road
Tingalpa Qld 4173
Australia
www.boolarongpress.com.au

First published 2023

A catalogue record for this book is available from the National Library of Australia

ISBN: 9781922643667 (Paperback)

Printed and bound by Watson Ferguson & Company, Tingalpa, Australia

DEDICATION

This book is dedicated to You,
because You can achieve any dream You have!

Dylan Alcott was born in Melbourne on
the 4th of December 1990. Dylan was born
with a tumour on his spinal cord. The tumour
was removed when he was a baby, but
it left Dylan a paraplegic and he needed
a wheelchair for the rest of his life.

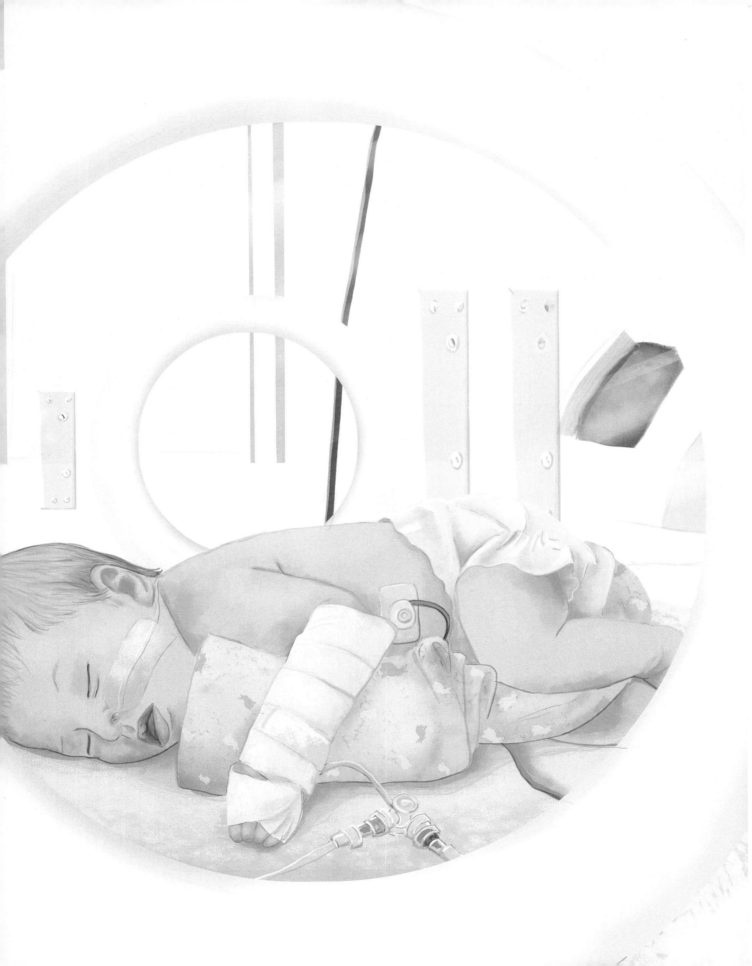

Like many kids, Dylan enjoyed sports and began to play wheelchair basketball and wheelchair tennis. Though Dylan was achieving great things in sports, he was sometimes being bullied by other kids who used to say nasty things to him because he was in a wheelchair. At times, Dylan felt sad that some kids would be mean to him. He had to try to stay positive and believe in himself, which sometimes wasn't easy to do.

As a child, Dylan was frustrated that he didn't see people on TV who were in wheelchairs like he was. There was no one in Parliament in a wheelchair, and people in the media weren't speaking about people in wheelchairs. There were millions of people in the world in wheelchairs, so why didn't we see them on TV? Dylan wanted to change that, and believed that he could change the way people saw and thought about people in wheelchairs.

At age twelve, Dylan went to a tennis tournament, but it wasn't the game of tennis that interested him the most. Dylan saw other people in wheelchairs just like him, which was exciting, as they were driving cars and doing things that Dylan thought weren't possible for him to do. By playing sport, Dylan felt that he was a part of the community.

When Dylan was fourteen, his best friend had a birthday party, but Dylan wasn't invited. Dylan felt disappointed, so he decided to go to his friend's house to ask him why he wasn't invited. Dylan thought it was because he was in a wheelchair, but his friend told him that he thought Dylan couldn't get into his party because of the stairs. Dylan realised that people needed to be better educated about people with disabilities.

Dylan had the rare ability to be great at two sports at the same time. At fifteen, Dylan made it into the Australian men's national wheelchair basketball team, which was called the Rollers. He first represented Australia at the 2006 Wheelchair Basketball World Championship, where the team won a bronze medal. At the 2008 Summer Paralympics, the Rollers won a gold medal. At seventeen, Dylan was the youngest person in the team. Wow! How amazing is that?

After his success at the Paralympics in basketball, Dylan returned to wheelchair tennis. Dylan had that fighting spirit in him that only the best athletes in the world have. He knew that with a lot of hard work and self-belief, he could achieve anything. In January 2014 in only his second professional tennis tournament, Dylan won the New Zealand Open. He now had his sights set on winning a Grand Slam tournament.

At the 2015 Australian Open, in front of his home crowd, Dylan defeated his opponent in straight sets to win the quad wheelchair Australian Open championship. Dylan knew that win would not only inspire himself and boost his confidence, but would also inspire kids around the world who were also in wheelchairs. He followed that up by winning the US Open, and that year he became the world's No. 1 ranked wheelchair tennis player.

In 2016, Dylan once again won the singles title at the Australian Open. Later that year, it was the Summer Paralympics Games, which were held in Rio de Janeiro, Brazil. In the Men's Quad Doubles, Dylan and his partner Heath Davidson defeated the reigning champions to win the gold medal. The following day, Dylan won the gold medal in the Men's Quad Singles. He was now a gold medallist in two different sports at the Paralympics.

When Dylan won his third Australian Open tennis championship in 2017, it was the first time that a wheelchair tennis match had been played on a Grand Slam centre court for a title. Millions of kids around the world saw Dylan on TV winning a Grand Slam.

Kids with disabilities began to think to themselves, "If Dylan can do it, then I can too."

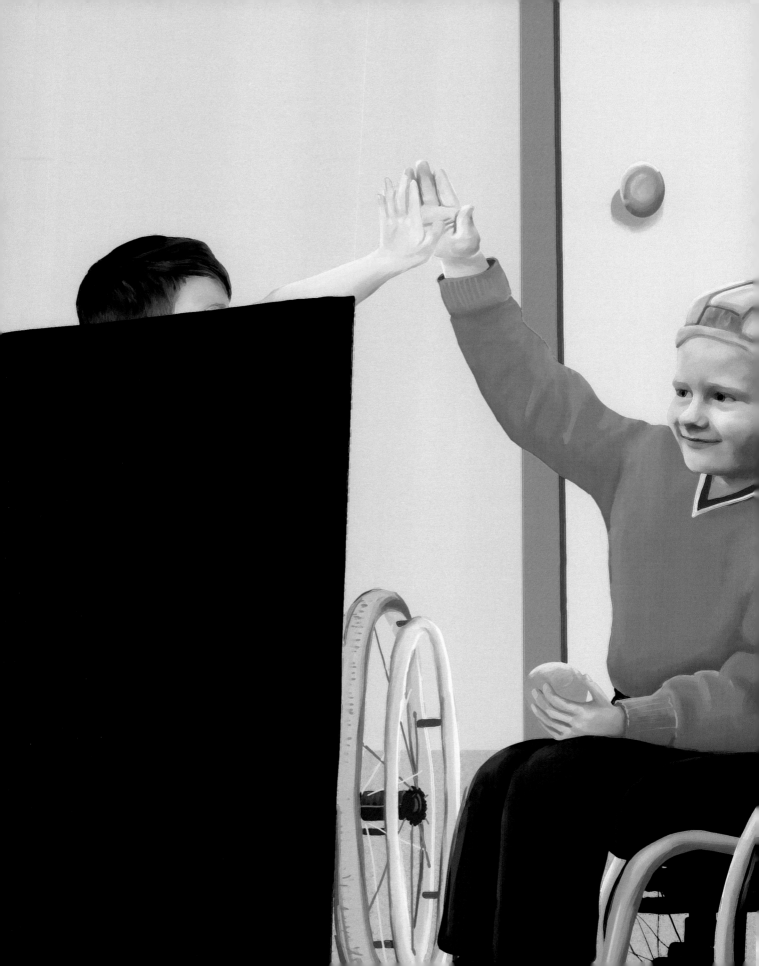

Dylan continued to win major tennis tournaments around the world. When he officially retired after the Australian Open in 2022, Dylan had won an incredible fifteen Grand Slam singles titles and eight Grand Slam doubles titles. Besides the Grand Slams, he also won another gold medal in the Quad Singles at the 2020 Summer Paralympics.

Though Dylan is retired from professional sports, he's kept himself very busy. He's a commentator on TV, works on radio, became a motivational speaker, and also runs the Dylan Alcott Foundation, which helps young Australians with disabilities. Phew! That's a lot, but that's not all. Dylan founded Ability Fest, which is a music festival that encourages anyone with a disability to come together to enjoy live music.

Dylan is a keen music fan, and even crowd surfed at a concert when he was twenty-four. Oh, and in 2022, Dylan was named Australian of the Year. Is there anything Dylan can't do?

To say that Dylan is a champion on and
off the court is an understatement.

He has shown all of us, whether we have
a disability or not, that anything is possible.

Any dream that you have can come true.
You simply cannot give up, you persevere, work
hard and continue to always believe in yourself.
And if somebody says you can't do something,
you just tell them that's not true, because
Dylan Alcott has shown us all that you can do
anything, you just have to believe in yourself.

FUN QUESTIONS

[1] What two sports did Dylan enjoy playing as a child?

[2] When Dylan was growing up, did he see lots of people in wheelchairs on TV?

[3] Why did Dylan's friend not invite him to his party?

[4] How old was Dylan when he won his first gold medal at the Summer Paralympics?

[5] Who won the 2015 quad wheelchair Australian Open championship?

[6] How many gold medals did Dylan win at the 2016 Summer Paralympics Games in Rio de Janeiro, Brazil?

[7] How many Grand Slam singles titles did Dylan win before he retired in 2022?

[8] What foundation does Dylan run?

[9] What did Dylan do at a concert when he was twenty-four?

[10] Who was the Australian of the Year in 2022?

ABOUT THE AUTHOR

Richard Simpkin was born in Sydney, Australia, in 1973 and has worked as a photographer in Australia, England and the US for 25 years.

He is a best-selling author of five books, two of which are about Australian legends who he met, photographed and interviewed.

In 2014, Richard also founded World Letter Writing Day, and has inspired children and adults all around the world to take a break from social media and write handwritten letters.

Richard has also conducted many workshops at schools in Australia. The students often ask him about many of the Australian legends that he has met over the years. This has inspired Richard to create these fun yet educational books about iconic Australians who we should all know about.

OTHER BOOKS BY AUTHOR

Australian Legends, 2005
Richard and Famous, 2007
100 Australian Legends, 2014
Michael in Pictures, 2015
Richard Simpkin Celebrity Quotes, 2016
Steve Irwin — Aussie Big Achievers, 2021
Cathy Freeman — Aussie Big Achievers, 2021
Ash Barty — Aussie Big Achievers, 2021
Shane Warne — Aussie Big Achievers, 2022

OTHER AUSSIE BIG ACHIEVERS BOOKS

AUSSIE BIG ACHIEVERS

STEVE IRWIN

written by RICHARD SIMPKIN   illustrated by DEBRA O'HALLORAN

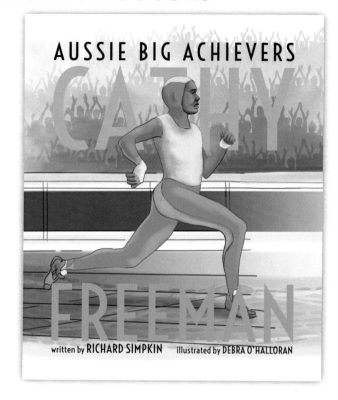

AUSSIE BIG ACHIEVERS

CATHY FREEMAN

written by RICHARD SIMPKIN   illustrated by DEBRA O'HALLORAN

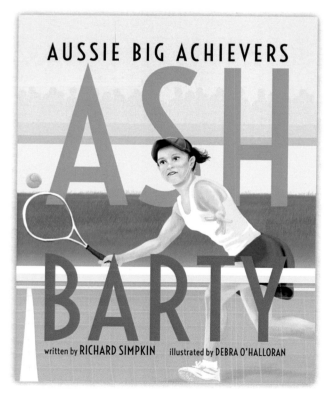

AUSSIE BIG ACHIEVERS

ASH BARTY

written by RICHARD SIMPKIN   illustrated by DEBRA O'HALLORAN

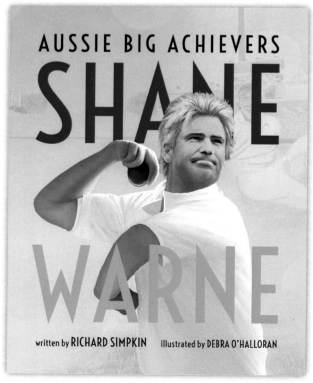

AUSSIE BIG ACHIEVERS

SHANE WARNE

written by RICHARD SIMPKIN   illustrated by DEBRA O'HALLORAN